Building Up Colonies

Building Up Colonies

The A. I. Root Co.
Medina, Ohio.
1907

Building Up Colonies

Building up colonies in anticipation of a honey-flow is one of the most important duties of a bee-keeper. There are some localities (not many, however) where nature does this work; but most of us have to anticipate nature carefully to some extent and do the work ourselves, or we get very little honey, or perhaps none at all. In this case the bee-keeper resembles a groom with a fine horse, who carefully studies its wants and by assiduously attending to these he gets the horse up to a point where everydody declares it is "as fit as a fiddle."

The same work can be performed for bees just before a honey campaign. It is not profitable to leave them to get ready of themselves; for when one does that, the honey-flow will be half over before the bees are ready for the work; and in some parts of the United States the flow would be all over with for the reason that it lasts not more than two weeks, whereas a month may be required to work up the bees to their maximum strength.

Before proceeding further it may be well to state that the "honey-flow" is the period during which the bees gather honey in excess of what they actually require for their own immediate uses. At other times they get only enough to keep them alive, or perhaps less.

The most successful honey-producers are those who know exactly when the bees will begin to gather a surplus; in fact, they know from experience almost to a day when the honey campaign begins, and accordingly have their hives overflowing with bees, and everything in readiness. They are like a train at the station, with steam up and blowing off at a throttle. Careless beekeepers, on the other hand, leave the bees to themselves, with the result that, when the time does come to get the honey, the bees are only half ready, or so weak in

Building Up Colonies

numbers that nothing can be done to get a crop of honey.

Quite frequently, also, they are short of hives and supers, etc., and may be seen running about looking for some brother bee-keeper who has been wise enough to lay in a stock of bee-supplies long before the time for using them.

Some farmers begrudge the time devoted to grooming the bees preparatory to a honey-flow or campaign; but there are few things which pay better than bee-keeping when properly attended to—certainly nothing on the farm pays better when the locality is in anywise favorable to the bees, and most places *are,* in the United States.

The management in localities differs, depending on the time when the main flowers are in bloom, so that it would be quite impossible to lay down any hard-and-fast rules for this work.

For example, in some parts of this country the surplus honey is secured in the fall of the year from buckwheat, aster, and goldenrod, in which instance one has all summer long in which to get prepared for the campaign. In other localities some succeed in getting a surplus of honey from apple-bloom, in which case the bee-keeper must be hustling at his work in early spring. A great many in the North get a crop from basswood in early summer; and if the basswood fails they get it later, perhaps, from clover-bloom.

The first thing to be done is to arrive at a clear understanding of the time when reasonable to expect a honey crop in the locality. If one knows this, and is quite sure of his point, the battle is half won, because, with a thorough knowledge of what one has to do, the work is well begun and is not apt to be slighted.

If it has been determined when the honey campaign will start, the work of grooming the bees ought to begin five or six weeks in advance. Now, it would be easy and very plain sailing to get the bees ready if it were not for the fact they sometimes swarm during this period; also, the weather may change and flowers may

Building Up Colonies

be conspicuous by their absence. Fruit-bloom frequently causes the bees to swarm, as the honey is not collected fast enough to allow of a surplus in the supers, and there is just enough of it to make the bees feel prosperous.

It would be well if we could so control the bees that they would not swarm, but, on the contrary, be content to remain in their own hive till each has from 100,000 to 150,000 bees. When a hive swarms, its prospects of yielding a fine surplus of honey are cut in two; for, as a rule, there is not sufficient time left to work up both the old colony and new to "fighting strength," with the net result the returns are as nothing compared with what they would have been had both been concentrated in one hive. The experienced reader may ask why this is so, and why the bees are so foolish as to throw away all their chances of hoarding up a crop. All we at present can say is that it is nature's plan. We on our part have to contend against nature or skillfully work nature's way to our own benefit.

The reason why swarming is a detriment to the honey-producer is this: When the colony swarms, the parent hive is left without a queen for nearly three weeks, which, of course, prevents it from making any progress. On the other hand, the swarm has to construct a new nest, and it is nearly a month before it gets any new bees, and before that time a considerable number of the bees die. Generally a good large swarm will accumulate a surplus during the period when the nest is being created, because the queen has not the full complement of combs to lay in: hence the young bees can not eat all the food gathered by the others. But it will be evident that if the two colonies, mother and daughter, had remained as one the chances of a large surplus of honey would be very much increased; consequently the most successful bee-keepers are those who are the most active in restraining the swarming instinct.

Swarming and honey-getting are therefore antagonistic to each other. Generally speaking, good bee-keep-

Building Up Colonies

are content to have sufficient new swarms to make up for those that may have died during winter and early spring. If one can do this he is an accomplished beekeeper, and does not require to read this booklet except as a pastime.

Getting the bees ready for fruit-bloom has already been dealt with in another booklet, entitled "Spring Management," so that we need not here reopen the question. Quite often during the fruit-blooming period the bees make great progress, the only requirement being that the weather be genial and pleasant, and that the hives be comfortable. As a rule the honey is not

One-and-one-half-story Hive

accumulated very fast; on the contrary, it comes in a manner to stimulate breeding to the utmost limit, with the result that the bees feel so very prosperous and numerous they make all preparations for swarming. In case the owner wishes to check the swarming fever, several courses are open to him.

One of the most effective and certainly the simplest methods of preventing swarms is simply to add a half-story to the hive. The bees are non-plussed by this move, as they have no alternative but to remain and fill up the vacancy for which they are at a loss to account. Some add the space below, but it is far easier

Building Up Colonies

to add from above and it is fully as effective as the other.

Others go a step further, and add a full story on the top, in which case it is practicable to take two or three of the well-filled frames from below and put them on the top. This puts a most effectual damper on the swarming fever.

A good many do not follow this plan because they believe adding so much room to the hive at this juncture would have a detrimental effect for the reason

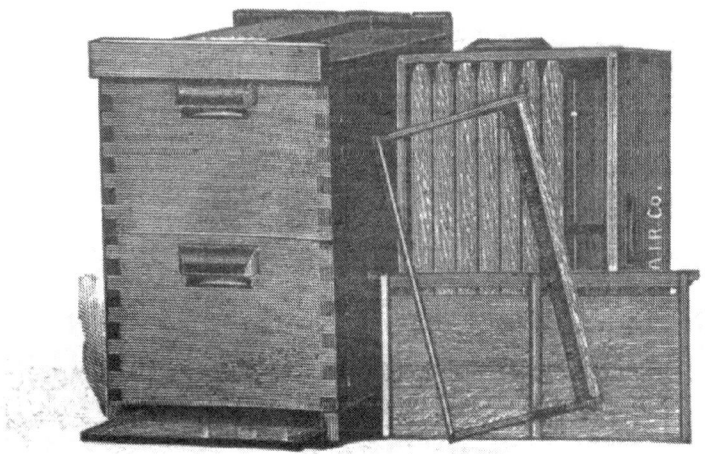

Two-story Hive.

there is apt to be a lull after the fruit-bloom season, and the bees have more room than they can conveniently take care of. In most cases this is not a valid objection, and to some extent can be remedied by using a half story on the top. Bees swarm when their hive is full or seems to be full. They can not stand prosperity.

It will not answer to add a half story containing section boxes with separators, holders, etc., because the bees do not regard that as an addition; on the contrary, the strange collection of small boxes seems to impel them to swarm, because the queen dislikes to use

Building Up Colonies

them for her purposes. It is different, however, when a super containing frames is added to the nest, for in this case the attention of the bees is attracted to the immense amount of work to be done before they may swarm, and they proceed in all haste to attend to the filling-up of the vacant space, which they seem to abhor.

If for any reason the bloom expected proves a failure the bee-keeper is, perforce, obliged to feed his bees; and the nearer he succeeds in imitating nature the better. First of all the syrup ought to be very thin, so as to

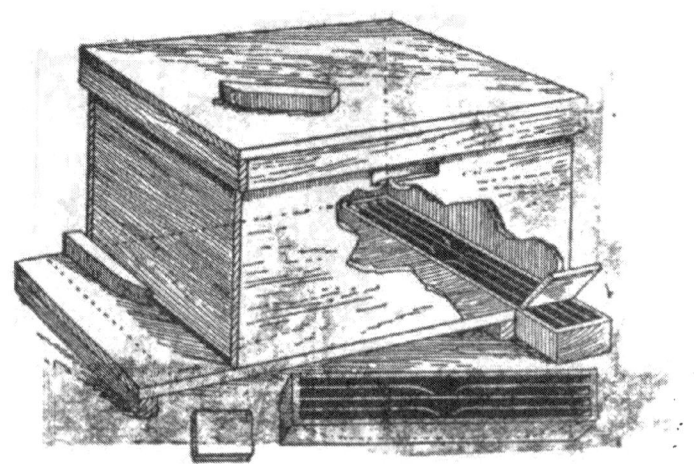

Alexander Feeder.

correspond with the nectar of flowers, and it should be fed often to stimulate the queen to laying at a great rate.

If the bees should swarm before the bee-keeper can stop them he can still save the situation by putting the swarm into a clean empty hive, placing it on the old stand with the parent colony on top of the new one, and a queen-excluder board in between. In this case the bees are in the same condition as those just outlined above. In a couple of weeks a colony of this kind

Building Up Colonies

will have a prodigious number of bees ready for the struggle.

Here it ought to be noted there is nought to be gained by having the bees ready too soon; but, as a rule, the honey season comes closely after the swarming season. In some cases the two seasons come together, in which event the main policy of the bee-keeper is to keep his bees from swarming by additions to the hive.

Even where comb honey in boxes is wanted, it is best to commence the season with a super for extracted honey and afterwards add the super with section boxes. This plan gets the bees in the habit of going above with their honey and storing it there rather than to put it in the brood-chamber, where it is not wanted. When the super with section boxes is put on, they are so much in the habit of going upstairs to deposit their loads they go to work on the boxes at once, apparently unaware of the change.

In some sections, the season is so late it really pays to make a "shook" swarm (presently to be described) from each colony, and thereby double the number of hives in the apiary. In this case very little feeding is necessary except in early spring, to induce the bees to swarm early. Possibly there may be a period between the time of swarming and the honey-flow when the bees may suffer from lack of food, and it should always be borne in mind that it takes five weeks to produce a worker-bee fit to go out into the fields to gather nectar.

It is not necessary to swarm bees naturally. One may make "shook" swarms, which are an imitation of natural swarms, and thereby save himself the bother and trouble incident to natural swarming. In this case the hive is opened; and if it appears to be in a condition bordering on swarming, the frame which has the queen adhering is lifted out and placed in a new hive fitted out with frames containing full sheets of foundation or combs. When the frame containing the queen has been placed in the hive, more bees are added by

Building Up Colonies

shaking each frame in a way to dump about two-thirds of the bees into the new hive.

Here we have a swarm which closely corresponds to a natural one. The two colonies may be placed near each other, or the two may be placed one on top of the other, with a queen-excluding honey-board between. The latter method suits a beginner better, as there is no trouble in having the bees abscond. Where the shook swarms are placed by themselves a goodly proportion of those so treated will abscond. The reason for this is found in the fact that the colony had no intention of swarming, and "shook" swarming *succeeds only when the bees have actually resolved on swarming themselves.* This method, it should be clearly understood, is successful only when natural swarming is imitated as closely as possible.

The plan is particularly useful in the case of *out-apiaries,* for natural swarming can not be depended on in this case, because no one is on hand to watch for the swarms, and many would be lost if left to their own devices.

If the apiarist prefers to allow natural swarming, the strength of the swarm may be kept up by placing the swarm alongside the mother colony for ten days, and then removing the parent elsewhere. This throws quite a number of fresh bees into the swarm and serves also to keep the mother weak.

Some go further, and, two weeks after the swarm issues, shake some bees from the mother on to the combs of the young colony, simply removing the top and shaking the bees from the frames right on to the section boxes of the younger. In this manner the swarm is kept to the maximum strength, and, of course, is ready for a honey-flow just as soon as it arrives. Methods of this kind may be modified to suit any emergency, and this one is mentioned merely to show what can be done.

Some get ready for the harvest by removing the queen with a frame of brood which is converted into a nucleus. This increases the apiary, as the nuclei are

Building Up Colonies

carefully nursed into good strong colonies before winter comes on. Of course, the colony so treated rears more queens; but this delays swarming; and in the time during which there is no queen the bees collect honey rapidly because they have no brood to feed. This succeeds best in localities where the honey season is short, say two or three weeks, during which period the bees have nought to do but gather honey, for it takes three weeks before they usually can have a laying queen.

Some cage the queen preparatory to the honey-flow, when they see there is quite enough bees and there is some danger of swarming. Some kill the queen just previous to a honey-flow, and thereby prevent swarming and excessive breeding during a very short honey season. They also secure young queens for the next year.

Others practice what is known as "equalizing," in which they take frames from the brood-chamber of the strong and give to the weak. This is not now considered good practice, and the tendency is to take from the weak and give to the strong. In this latter case one gets a number of powerful colonies that do far more work than a number of moderately strong ones. So long as we can keep them from swarming, it is the tremendously big colonies that do the work of honey-collecting; and the most successful bee-keeper is he who can have great big colonies and yet keep swarming in check.

The following, by Mr. Alexander, the famous New York bee-man, will serve to give in relief some other methods of getting ready:

Rearing Queens for Early Increase

During the past few weeks I have received several letters requesting me to state through *Gleanings* just how we rear our queens so as to have them laying in time to make a large increase early in the season.

First, by way of explanation I will say that, in order to do this we stimulate our bees by early feeding to early breeding, so we have many strong colonies quite early in the season; and in recommending this I am well aware that some very good bee-keepers prefer to have their colonies only of medium strength until about the commencement of their harvest for

E. W. Alexander's Apiary of 750 Colonies.

Building Up Colonies

surplus. But as we handle our bees quite differently in many ways from some, we try hard to have all the strong full colonies we can as early as possible, and we seldom keep a queen after she is two years old. We supersede them some time during their third summer. This necessitates killing about one-third every year.

Now, after taking them from their winter quarters we walk along in front of our hives and count how many we have that are two years old. This is very easily done, for the little tin tag on the front of each hive tells us at a glance the age of the queen in the hive. These colonies we now give especial attention to, we feed them regularly, and rather more at a time than we do the colonies that have younger queens. We also frequently give them frames of hatching brood from other colonies and at all times try to keep them as warm as we can. In this way we have no trouble in building them up strong and full of brood early in May; and while we are doing this we insert frames of comb that have some drone comb in near the middle of the two or three hives we wish to rear drones from to mate with our early queens. This should be done about ten days before we start the rearing of queen-cells. Then about May 15 we borrow the bees from several of our strongest colonies for one day to start our queen-cells, as is now practiced by Mr. Pratt, of Swarthmore, Pa., which I consider the finest way to start the rearing of choice queens of any thing I have ever tried, as we have to use these bees only one day, then we give them their queen and brood, which leaves them in about as good condition as they were in before they were disturbed. When we counted up our old queens we found we had about 200 to be superseded. Now, this will require 400 young queens if we divide each one; then we have about 100 colonies that have younger queens that we wish to divide. They will require 100 more, so we find that we shall need some 500 young queens to make our increase and supersede our old queens. Then we should allow about 50 for those that are lost, so we will start the rearing of about 600 cells. We would much rather have more cells and queens than we can use than to be short only a few. As soon as this is done we go to half the colonies that have two-year-old queens and kill their queens, *also* destroy any eggs or larvæ they may have in any queen-cells. Then we go to the boxes that have our newly started cells in, and take out five or six cells for each colony that has been made queenless. These we insert near the center of their brood, and they will soon build them out into as nice cells as we ever saw. Then about two days before these cells are ready to hatch we kill the remaining old queens; then we tier up with two hives of combs all the queenless colonies we have. But be sure you divide the combs of brood and honey that are in the hive below about equal so each one of the three will have some brood and honey. Then insert one of these nearly ripe queen cells into each one of the hives as they stand on top of each other, and put a queen-excluder between each two hives; also

11

Building Up Colonies

have a separate entrance for each hive that the queen may use when she goes out to mate. You see, aside from the queen the colony has access to each one of the three hives through the excluders. In this way you will soon have three nice young laying queens in nearly every colony that contained your old queens. Then to use up our surplus queen-cells we form nuclei by taking one or two frames of honey or brood and about a quart of bees, and put them into an empty hive, and set them near the hive we take the brood and bees from so as to give them back to the old colony as soon as the young queen is mated. In this way we have no trouble in rearing and in having fertilized all the young queens we care for to make our increase and supersede all our old queens at the same time.

After you have practiced this method of rearing queens you will have no trouble in having all you want ready to use for early increase some time before there is any harvest of surplus honey in our Northern States.

With us this method of rearing early queens is so easy that we frequently have more than we can use. Sometimes we have 30 or more full colonies in our apiary that contain two or three laying queens each, nearly all summer, until we can find or make a place to use them. They make a fine colony to draw brood from. When there are two or three good queens in a three-story hive the bees all work from one entrance as one colony; for as soon as the young queens commence to lay we close up the entrance that was made for them to fly from, and they all work together.

Some of you may want to know what I would do if my queens were all young and I had none I cared to kill. In that case I would do the same with the colonies as in the case with the old queens, only I would save these younger queens in nuclei until I could use them in making increase.

We manipulate our bees so much through May and June that it is no uncommon thing for us to make 100 or more new colonies, mostly nuclei, to-day, for some special purpose, and then in a few days unite the most of them again with other colonies. We can do this very easily, as we use our common hives and combs for all this work.

In the article I wrote for the Dec. 1st *Gleanings* I made some assertions as to what might be made from 100 colonies in a year providing we gave them the best of care. Since then I have received some letters that show the writers think I am in a tight place, and can not rear the necessary queens in time to make as early increase as I advise. To those doubting Thomases I wish to say that we can rear *twice* as many queens as is necessary to double our colonies before June 10; and I assure you if you handled *your* bees as we sometimes handle ours, all that I have ever claimed *can be done*. Many beekeepers seem to think that, if they set their bees out of the cellar about April 1, that is all there is to do until they hive some swarms and put on their clamps of empty sections. We find about as much to do from the time they are set out up to Aug. 1, when we commence to extract, as we do when we are

Building Up Colonies

extracting; and there is no slack time. The bees are kept busy every day, either to rear queens, make increase, form nuclei, draw out foundation, or something that is necessary to be done by them in order to be in proper condition for our August harvest. We usually spend the last week in July uniting all weak colonies and nuclei with stronger swarms so as to have the yard well cleaned up of those that are not in condition to give us a good surplus. Then we can give all our attention to extracting and caring for our surplus honey.

In conclusion let me assure you that there is not much danger of having your colonies too strong in bees at any time if you will use them as you should, for they are the principal factor in making your business a success. We like them in the spring to rear those nice early queens from. We like them to make our increase from. We like them to get our surplus from. Yes, my friends, and there is a pleasure in putting away good, strong, full colonies in their winter quarters, as you would put money away in the bank to draw an income from in the future.

The position taken by Mr. Alexander on feeding syrup to bees ought to be noted, for feeding judiciously means strong, powerful colonies just when most wanted. Of course, the beginner may feed the bees too early or too late for the honey-flow. The syrup is converted into great masses of bees ready, like a powerful army, for a vigorous campaign.

As has been already suggested, it is better not to double up before the honey-flow comes but wait to do that when it has come, and not before. Then when the day has arrived to gather in the honey crop weak colonies are united till every hive is fairly overloaded with bees.

One may and probably will vary the Alexander method to suit his conditions, because he has one month more than most of us to get ready for the struggle, and that makes a vast difference in making ready.

In some places where the season is extra early and the price of honey is good, some import bees from the South to make up for winter losses. Two fine frames of bees added to a weak colony is a grand acquisition; and the only question to consider is: Is it too expensive? The frames ought to be added before fruit-bloom comes to be most useful, for it frequently happens that the only reason why bees do not gather a sur-

Building Up Colonies

plus from fruit-bloom is because they are not numerous enough. Fruit-trees are being more extensively planted than ever before in the history of the world.

This business of getting honey from fruit-bloom would be greatly facilitated if we could secure bees cheaply from the South. At present the express rates are too high for a traffic of this kind; but it seems probable that, in the future, a large trade will be done in sending bees in early spring to Northern apiarists. We of the North could produce bees by means of feeding syrup far cheaper than we could ever purchase them; but we can not, except in some instances, get them soon enough for the fruit-bloom. In buying bees from the South we desire them early to put into the hives soon after the winter is over. This method is worthy of consideration wherever there is a large amount of early fruit-bloom. One may not quite succeed in getting a crop of fruit-bloom honey, but it is quite possible in many instances to get the section combs drawn out ready for the honey-flow from basswood, locust, or white clover, later in the season.

In order to give the reader as many plans as possible to think over I will give that of Mr. Doolittle, one of the most successful bee-keepers this country has produced. The best way would be to devise a method suited to the special circumstances of the apiarist.

Doolittle's Methods

In order to produce good results in comb honey, the first requisite is plenty of bees when the honey harvest arrives, for whatever else we may have, success can not be obtained without plenty of bees. Again, as I said before, these bees must be on hand in time for the honey harvest, else they become merely consumers instead of producers. How often we find men keeping bees on this (consuming) plan, getting nothing from them in the line of surplus honey, unless it is some little buckwheat honey, or that gathered from fall flowers, which is generally of inferior quality, for the reason that they do not have anything but colonies weak in bees at the time the harvest of white honey occurs! Such bee-keeping does not pay, and for this reason I have dwelt thus long on this part

Building Up Colonies

to enable all to see that, of all others, this is the most important item in the production of comb honey.

Our first step, then, is to produce plenty of bees in time for the honey harvest. With most of us white clover is the main honey-producing plant, which blooms about June 15th to 20th, and by June 25th is at its best; hence, our bees must be in readiness at that time if we wish to succeed.

From practical experience I find that it takes about six weeks to build up an ordinary colony in the spring to where they are ready to produce honey to the best advantage; so I commence to stimulate brood-rearing about the first of May. I have tried many plans of feeding, both in the open air and in the hive, to stimulate brood-rearing, but finally gave them all up for the following: When I have decided that it is time to commence active operations for the season, I go to each colony and look them over, clipping all queens' wings that were not clipped the previous season, and equalize stores so that I know each colony has enough honey to carry it at least two weeks without any fear of starvation. At this time I find, as a rule, each good colony will have brood in four or five combs, the two center combs containing the largest amount. I now reverse the position of these combs of brood by placing those on the outside in the center of the brood-nest, which brings the combs having the most brood in them on the outside. Thus, while the colony has no more brood than it had before, the queen finds plenty of empty cells in the center of the brood-nest, in combs having some brood in them, and she at once fills these combs with eggs, so that in a few days they will contain more brood than those that were removed to the outside, while the bees have fed and taken care of this as well as though its position had not been changed. Thus quite a gain has been made in regard to increasing the brood.

In about eight days, if the weather is favorable, the whole yard is gone over again, and this time a frame of honey is taken from the outside of the cluster, and the cappings to the cells broken by passing a knife flatwise over them, when the brood-nest is separated in the center, and this frame of honey, thus prepared, placed therein.

As I go over the yard each time, I am careful to know that each colony has abundant honey to last them at least two weeks; for if we wish to obtain the largest amount of brood possible, the bees must never feel the necessity of feeding the brood sparingly on account of scanty stores. It is also necessary to know that there are no cracks or open places at the top of the hive to let the warm air pass out of the hive, but tuck all up as nicely as you would your bed on a cold winter's night.

After seven days more have elapsed I again go over the whole yard and insert another frame of honey in the center of the brood-nest prepared as before. If at any time I am short of honey I use sugar-syrup made by taking confectioners' A sugar and dissolving it in hot water (at the rate of one pound of water to two pounds of sugar), by placing the two in an

Building Up Colonies

extractor-can, which should be placed some three or more feet from the floor. Stir well till all is dissolved. Now procure an old pan of the ordinary size and punch the bottom full of holes about 1-16 of an inch in diameter, punching the holes from the inside of the pan, when it should be placed under the faucet of the can containing the syrup. Immediately under the pan place another can if you have it (if not, a washtub will answer), and you are ready for business. Take an empty comb and lay it down flat under the pan and on the bottom of the can, when you will open the faucet, letting the syrup out in the pan till enough has run out to fill one side of your comb, when you will shut it again. Turn over your comb and fill the other side, and after hanging in your tin comb-bucket (wash-boiler, or some convenient tin thing which is almost always at hand) a little while to drain, it is ready to be used in any spot or place, the same as a frame of honey. I prefer this way of feeding to any feeder in existence.

If you wish to make quick work of filling these combs, have an assistant to hand you the empty combs and take the filled ones; roll up your sleeves and hold the combs near the bottom of the can, or low enough down so the falling syrup will force the air out of the cells so they will be filled; turn your faucet so the required amount of syrup will be in the pan all the time, and you can fill them (the combs) almost as fast as the assistant can hand them to you. The sides of the can keep the syrup from spattering about the room, and what is caught therein can be turned into the upper can again.

The next time I go over the yard I generally reverse the brood as at first, as well as to put a frame of honey in the center. By this time the bees will have hatched out of the combs which were placed on the outside; and as the queen does not lay as readily on the outside of the cluster, these combs will not be as well filled as the center ones.

After about a week more, the yard is gone over again in like manner; and if but nine frames are used to the hive, this time will conclude the stimulating process, for at the end of about five days more, or about the 10th of June, all our frames are full of brood, and our colonies in good condition for receiving the surplus boxes.

Several years ago when I wished to unite weak colonies in the spring I did so early in the season, for the "books" said that the time to unite was when it was discovered that two colonies were too weak to be of use alone, which generally happened in April. That uniting two weak colonies to make one strong one is profitable to the apiarist, no one will deny (unless, perchance, we are obliged to use everything in the shape of bees, as we were in 1882, in order to get our former number back again after a heavy loss); still, that uniting must make the one better than either of the two would have been when the honey harvest arrives, or our labor of uniting is worse than useless. After practicing the plan given in the books for a year or two, I became convinced that colonies thus formed were no better, at the end of two or three weeks, than

Building Up Colonies

each one would have been had they been left separate. I have put as many as seven remnants of colonies together, in April, the seven making a good large colony at the time, and in a month all were dead. After coming to the conclusion that I could not unite bees with profit in early spring, I adopted the following plan, which has proved successful so far:

About the middle of April, some cool evening, I look over all my bees by removing the cap and raising the quilt a little, so that I can see how strong in bees the colonies are, and all that do not occupy five spaces between the combs are marked, and the first warm day are shut on to as many combs as they have brood in, and a division-board placed in the hive, so as to contract the hive to suit the size of the colony. Honey enough is provided to keep them amply for two weeks, and the rest of the combs I store away for safe keeping, unless some of the strongest of them are able to protect them from robbers, in which case I leave them outside of the division-board, so that the bees can carry honey from them as they wish. The entrances are contracted so as to let but one bee pass at a time, for the smallest colonies, while the larger ones do not have more than one inch in length of the entrance given them.

The next work is to increase the brood as fast as possible in these small colonies. I keep them shut on the combs first given them till they are filled with brood clear down to the bottom, before they are given more room. As soon as this is accomplished I give them a comb of honey prepared as before described, placing it between two full combs of brood. In about a week this comb will be filled with brood as full as the others. I go over them once a week in this way till I have five frames of brood in the strongest, when I take a frame of brood just hatching out, from those having five full frames, and give it to the next strongest, say one that has four frames, putting a frame of honey in the place where it came from. Thus I keep working till all of them contain five frames of brood, which should occur from the 10th to the 15th of June in this locality. I now go to No. 1 and open it, looking the frames over till I find the one the queen is in, when it is set outside, and the four remaining frames and all the adhering bees are taken to No. 2. I then spread the five frames in No. 2 apart, so as to set the four frames brought from No. 1 in each alternate space made by spreading the frames in No. 2. No. 2 is now closed up, and in a few days it is ready for the boxes. It will eventually make as good a colony for storing in boxes as the best of the stronger ones; at least, such has been my experience so far. I have never known bees to quarrel, nor a queen to be harmed by this plan of uniting, as the bees are so completely mixed up that they do not know what to fight about.

But to return to No. 1, where the queen and frame of brood were left standing outside of the hive. I now place this frame of brood back in the hive and put an empty frame beside it, adjusting the division-board, and I have a nice nucleus from which to get a queen to be used in swarming, as given further

Building Up Colonies

on. Many of the old bees carried to No. 2 will return, thus making a strong nucleus, which will fill the empty frame with nice, straight worker comb in a few days, and still another if the queen is left long enough.

Now. if I wish no increase of colonies during the season I serve my whole apiary as I did Nos. 1 and 2, beginning early enough to be sure that none have brood in more than five frames, by putting boxes on the strongest just before apple-blossoms, and a few boxes are often filled from this source, as the bees must work in boxes if at all, when shut on five frames. It will be seen that I use nine frames to the hive; but the plan is the same with any number of frames. This having every frame in a hive crowded to the fullest capacity with brood two weeks before the height of the honey harvest has much to do with a good yield of honey, I assure you. This is the condition I aim to have all my bees in, and I have tried to tell you how so you can do the same, if you wish to adopt the plan I follow.

THE ADVANTAGES OF BUYING
Root's
Bee-keepers' Supplies

Quality
They are well made from good material. You are never disappointed or disgusted on receiving goods inaccurately cut, and roughly made, from inferior stock.

Interchangeableness
This accuracy with which goods are made allows a customer to order goods year after year, and each lot will fit the others as new parts fit in repairing an Elgin watch.

Promptness
With our immense manufacturing facilities, the adoption of standard goods, and the establishment of agencies and branch houses throughout the various parts of the country, we can get goods to you with wonderful promptness.

Cost
No goods of like quality are sold at lower prices than we sell them, while the shipping of them in car lots to the branch houses and agencies allows the customer to get them at factory prices within a short distance of his home. Send for a catalog and list of dealers, and save freight and time by ordering from your nearest dealer.

CPSIA information can be obtained
at www.ICGtesting.com
Printed in the USA
BVHW031656270722
643176BV00008B/286